BRIDLED

Amy Meng

BRIDLED

PLEIADES
PRESS

The Lena-Miles Wever Todd Poetry Series

Warrensburg, Missouri

Library of Congress Control Number:
ISBN 978-0-8071-6889-9
Copyright © 2018 by Amy Meng

Published by Pleiades Press

Department of English
University of Central Missouri
Warrensburg, Missouri 64093

Distributed by Louisiana State University Press

Cover Image: Stas Orlavski, "Figure with Butterflies," Charcoal, graph-
ite, ink, xerox, transfer and collage on paper laid on canvas. 48 x 36.
2005

Book design by Sarah Nguyen
First Pleiades Printing, 2018

Financial support for this project has been provided by the University
of Central Missouri and the Missouri Arts Council, a state agency.

Table of Contents

Acknowledgements

For my family.

And a reminder to my future selves.

ORPHEUS, ASYMPTOTE

I've tasted bones from the butcher's

house and once a sun-bleached fragment

of skull. The longer I live the closer I get.

At rush hour turnstiles click like a summer

mob of beetles — their shining mouths.

Trains deafen as they speed, departure

trailing like a loosened bow.

Inside the car it's quiet, silent

inside speed and delicious

to be with something that just holds me.

By the lane birches are notched with public initials:

it seems like proof but isn't.

Nights, my bare thigh bumps a table and pain

spreads like slow ink. I move

through the exercises of lust,

a sour drill: look at tight buds

of lavender, the ring finger

of strangers: look at people getting into

their homes, light from the hallway falling

flat on their faces — it's never enough. I turn

and walk straight into the blazing X of the sun.

IF I EXIST THE EQUATION GETS MORE DIFFICULT

Night turned into itself with devotion.
I delineated my shape with the dotted
precision of a coupon, meaning

I could no longer be mistaken
for a knot of gasps.
It's true no one requested this

but it's what I submitted.
On the couch I waited for the lover
to come home —

work being his big world.
The stovetop fan whirred like a low, fat
tongue and I imagined our children

at the dinner table, though I hope
dreaming did not make them so.
I received many gifts of aprons

which hung like bats around the kitchen.
I inventoried grains in the pantry, discs of blue
toilet cleaner. The parts of me not dedicated

to counting never re-appeared
though I waited with growing alarm.
My mother said This is how it is

and I believed her.
I remembered summers of walking
in front of buses, biking headlong

down stairwells: death was a frog
in science class. Now stillness
held me in a shadow box.

I leafed through the days
like a practice test, thinking
someday I'd be twisted open

into real time. Because I was a girl,
I listened. I thought life
was the thing you got right:
clean as the camera's flooding flash.

GOOD IS WHAT YOU BECOME WHEN YOU THINK SOMEONE IS LOOKING

In movie theaters I knew what love felt like: saw it spin
the car in a sharp U towards the latched front door,
saw its tender underside, its doing
without being watched —
though of course I was watching, all of New York
was watching, and we were in thrall: staked
to our plush seats with belief running cold as marrow.
I wanted to be together on the sidewalk, together
at the farmer's market, two shark fins cruising.
Ogling radishes, noticing the girls' wet hair
bare their skulls like bulbs of scallions:
I wanted our brains to be holding hands.
I was learning so fast and so good,
I was a stalagmite of knowledge.
Love was a street of grand openings,
racks of copper pots dinging in the kitchen,
a sweep of automatic lights coming on one by one
— gently, like touch.
Who knew about after the wedding,
inside the vague formula of marriage. I yearned
like this was the last, best toy in the crackerjack box.

RECOVERY

In those days thought hung
like one rotted bulb of light
quiet and cold past glowing.

I loved a man who moved
over me: a horsehair bow
bent on still and silent strings.

Each morning sour cans lined
the shelves and my eyes slid oily over.
We smoked naked at windows

and swallowed oysters
for breakfast, greedy as salt
biting tongue.

I lost track of myself, but nothing else
seemed to forget what it was.
The street remained a hard back;

the accident on my leg
healed into a muted seam.
I wanted love to be an end

to the days, which I kept
walking through door after door.
Some nights the man hauled

into wakefulness.
I looked in him for something more
than mere sensation,

which is what ghosts are.
That searching was almost
like being seen.

NEARLY

Light, which I dreamt was a decoder
of everything, falls

uneven in piles on snowdrifts.
A final loose lasso of geese flies:
south, southeast.

Someone sleeps in the next room,
his breath curt stutters.

Inside I look at a book of mosaics:
shattered bones recomposed.
The abbreviated glass resolves

into horses,
an evening lake.

It is so pleasurable to recognize strangers
— the brain likes this little glory,
moment to crow over.

Lately I recognize myself more and more
like an explanation stepping out

from the woodwork of fact.
I am special and irrevocable,
under the skin of skin of stone.

Whoever is in the next room stirs and creaks
in sleep. The sound of his motion rearranges me.

SONG

It was the year of *Sorry, ma'am, we're out.*
Year the drill sergeant yelled *Dive!*
and the splash of thirty bodies obeyed.

Year of nails cleaving two–by–fours
to broken windows, of politely lifting
skirts over a man asleep on the tracks.

Year of chair shadows and fern shadows
stretching across the room while I never
left my bed.

Are you there? I said, and the trap sprang
upon the mouse's neck. Bone china shook
a little on the shelves.

It was the year of corn steaming
sweet on the stove, trout flipping
fat–bellied onto our plates.

Year of bend our necks and give thanks.
Year of put that wine down and kiss me.

Year the cake wouldn't rise, year the sun
wouldn't go down, year the drill sergeant
said *Sing,* and the soldier said *Sir what song.*

ROUTINE

Our mailbox with its tiny key. Your hand rising
   to the low archway, unthinking. White noise
machine playing rain over rain
   and warm thunder as humidity flattened us
into damp sleep. Beers ringed our shelves and outside:
   bodegas lousy with swimming noodles
and steel wool. I watched you chop bouquets
   of parsley and felt fed, your constant division
of thought clean as the slash of an oar.
   Overhead moths flashed
like a handkerchief shaken in semi-darkness.
   The books damp. My elbows sliding
roughly across the couch. Your neck sticky
   in August, hands ringing me
awake for the next meal. Your visiting my body
   just to see it there, sudden brightening
against the terra cotta pots;
   your heading towards me,
checking my stomach for pain; your cradling,
   which could be considered dancing
in another house—

saxophone in its clean case

    you never played for me,

sink coated in oil, ring

    around the tub I couldn't scrub out;

burner's weak wrist

    of flame, avocados molding

in a bowl; floorboards rotted enough

    to hear neighbors' whispers, air

conditioner finally blaring: our room, our bed:

    the place we went to close

our eyes and vanish next to each other.

ON DISTANCE

I tell the lover: dig me up

like a field. I say there are bodies inside.

It seems he can only offer the usual

kind of tenderness. What I call need

is so yawning — I think it is something new.

I say it's bravery to sink

like seeds into ground, knowing

you'll be forgotten.

I ask him to sing like a soldier alone.

Finally he touches me

out of pity for himself, to untether

the line of my needing.

Outside the wind, at least, can't lie.

Though the body can and does.

SELF-GUIDED

I'm told thought passes like a long afternoon
of traffic. The freeway in Cape Canaveral,

for instance: car after car shredding
outside the roadside diner, gravity's

thousand knuckles bearing down
as your family apologizes for the view,

the heat, the sound.
Cokes with sloppy lemon wedges sweat

between us. Pay attention
to where breath moves, how air throttles

and snags in lung, how I feel
like a bad cell — like a flock of bad cells.

The sandwich falls to shreds. A tide
of cars pulls over us. Astonishing

how neatly distance hides, tucked
like a kerchief. I'm told I get closer

by not trying so hard. If I lose count
I can start again from one.

PERMISSION

Those years blur like stacked wax sleeves of crackers.

It didn't work, it was obvious as starched linen whipping on a mast.

I was used to measuring
my life against anything other than itself.
Can you accept this by way of explanation?

Sometimes he baked bread and as it cooled
we hovered to hear its crackling, our ears turning close
as sister flowers.

Sometimes he looked at me like I was a dawn.

I thought to leave there had to be nothing
left, but always something shows
what it was.

Planes out of Newark skimmed overhead.
Tomatoes on the fire escape tightened in their skins through the night.

If you need a sign, I want to say. Make it any of these.

MOTION, MOVED

I fold into the cold croissant of bed.
When he leaves I flutter open

like a valve. His wardrobe,
my hangers, our chest

of drawers: possession
tossed like a rule

over everything. He says:
I think you should move out.

My deed wiped away like light
snow from the car window.

The last time we touched
was an accident in sleep.

I think of the shout
of a shot in hunting season

and stay down
in the leaves of bed.

I feel close and protective of my brain,
which is already doing things for me.

Staring down the mattress edge, I tell myself:
Swing over. Render unto Caesar what is Caesar's.

AFTER MAINE

The suddenness of our shame
surprised me: putting doors

between our undressed bodies, my private
names stoppered in his mouth.

Never mind that you can't stop knowing,
can only wait for it to die.

I loved him most when he was all child:
dancing towards me like a stork,

beeping at me in the bathroom,
clamping cold feet under my knees

without apology.
To survive I became a blank

screen. Underneath the screen
a jumble of wires, remembering.

SUMMER I DIDN'T HAVE

I walked down to Charlie,
the fish man, who twisted open
live clams and tilted

them into my mouth.
My mother called and I treated her
to mint gelato in the town gazebo.

We listened to rose-brass trombones step
through the octaves.
When the carnival came, I went.

A calliope's jingle threaded
the Ferris wheel, its rusted red
buckets, while the pop of BB guns

struck tin rabbits.
I ate funnel cake peel by peel, tacky
with confectioner's sugar.

Sundays, I swilled the park's greeny air.
No need to count and re-count
my selves: what was mine

was certainly mine.
Those were days full of humming
without realizing I was making a song.

My legs straightened in a bathtub
of clean water, breath sliding sideways:
home. Final inning. August.

I'd never felt so safe.

EACH SEASON THE EYE OF THE DEER IS RE-PINNED TO A DIFFERENT FACE

If suffering is an eclipse
as I once thought
then beneath it is forest.

Rivers exist as steady
sound. The warm–blooded
eaters pausing.

ADAPTATION

He's thinking about leaving me
or else he's already left.

A mystery how anything ever gets done.

Owls tune their throats
in the magnolias, the sky petrified to a white

plank planes move along.

Pulling crumbs off the table in one short arc:
I know the room I want to be, but not where it is.

The patio's wind chimes are beautiful

because they are changed. So I whet
myself into the sharp heat of a penny on the boardwalk.

Soon I will be unafraid,

even of the sun
following me through the years.

SO IT'S OVER, YOU SAID

I studied you with a camera's dead-on
closing shot

as you severed with singular effort:

a fisherman flinging back his weighted line.
A soldier's brusque and violent mercy.

SOMETIMES THE NIGHTMARE IS THAT IT DIDN'T HAPPEN

The hero wakes from her happiness,
which was a dream.

The late night meals were not real:
not the sweet notes tucked

around the house, or the other's
breathing in bed like a compass.

The list goes on and she rises
into her new life, believing

she could have been so mistaken.
She sees the vividness

of the freeway, the lettering
on coupon books,

each decimal biting
the soft ash of paper.

And sometimes the nightmare is
that it all repeats:

breakfast cooks. Kettle boils.
Our hero's dream swings

like an axe past her ear.
Across the city

lines of diamonds
flash in soft black cases.

WALKING THROUGH THE PARK

I find a set of bones. They seem
like bat wings becoming
whale fins becoming a blurred human
hand, waving in a photo.

The photo is of me. I'm naked in bed
and saying *Hi* through the lens, where your eye
crinkles as you snap the shot. The photo
in the phone you use to call home and ask about your dog.

I hear your dog
barking through the computer screen.
I hear loons cast their calls
in a wide arc through the night.

The night around you becomes the weighted
net thudding around me. A woman's voice slices
open my sleep. She calls for help like a bellows deflating.
Someone yells: *what's wrong?*

Something is wrong with the scale
of this scene. Ants giant, purple worms belching,
bloated with blood from some war. I am in the soil,
my face like an opened apple.

I uprooted something in the dirt.
Maybe it was already seized
by rot, ready to dissemble at a touch. Maybe
it was a pale shoot just about to bloom.

In the park I touch a carriage
of bones, complete as a silver tea set.
I hear an animal chased across trees,
always on the brink of remembering why.

TONIGHT NOBODY IS COLD

Lately I've longed
for forest with every
table leg I see,

rubbed each possible
name smooth
as a shark's tooth.

In my stomach, expectation
lights up bright and solid
as the carcass of a buffalo

in the American West:
one day I will be
like a parent

creating a flash-lit trail
through the dark and open–
faced grass.

I shepherd the hours,
their warm bodies
like lambs through a gate.

Maybe I will be good
by the time you arrive.

DINNER

I pare memory
carefully, until he emerges
like the hard-earned heart
of an artichoke.

AFTER MAINE

A sound drops through

the slot of understanding

and everything comes

into sharp focus.

To leave he made me ugly:

after all, beauty is the leash.

We did the favor of seeing

each other clearly, though

never at the same time.

The monkey statuettes, mason jars

of grain, each vinyl sleeved

in a jacket I dusted: I moved it at all

over the years like a slow dance:

me and the house, this form

I could hammer and open and shatter

glasses in without much changing.

The windowpanes held still

but outside: things appeared

and erased themselves

brutally, like fun.

INSIDE-OUT JOKE

There was never a man with ribs like a bear
whose shucked glasses left his face raw
and tender as a nerve.
He never lifted the gentle brand
of love to me to see how I wore it.
I made our bed disappear like a lungful of air
divided among the cells.
He drew across me like a rock igniting.
It was difficult for me to be so new.
It was difficult to be cancelled like a light.
I've kept the lace of memory
in absolute darkness. Now I wish
I remembered whether you held
my hand and how.

AFTER SIGNING THE LEASE ON MY NEW APARTMENT

In a maze the string is the clue.
Yet still it ends
as though I'd gotten outside of something.

HE TELLS ME: COME BACK WHEN YOU'VE PRIED YOURSELF OPEN

Of course I won't
though the thought moves
like radar through my bones.

I've waited on the cinderblock
steps, in the piss-filled alleyway,

to be let in. My legs kept
moving though my ear was pinned
to waiting.

If I want to be touched I'll go outside
where each thing kisses me —

even the cat's teeth.
In the wind everything waves, everything
points in the same direction

like a watch of sailors
at attention. I call to myself

in a shepherd's high voice:
by my count I'm almost gathered.
The trees hesitantly put on their leaves.

The rain that held itself all day
comes down suddenly, like applause.

AFTER MAINE

I knew.

I had known almost since the beginning
the way I looked at Carla, the neighbor girl,
and saw her laughing like an unlatched

door, caught the whiff
of danger in her house
like gasoline, wetness
you can't identify.

One afternoon I saw it all in a sudden crush:
her parents moving through the unlit den,
her bedroom curdled with silence.

This is how, when you turned away,
I heard you like thunder
sounding between the channels of sleep.

But in my house I had many drawers
and put knowing away
like an ornament, a knife.

AGAINST MYSELF

I know what I'll do, though I wish
I'd do anything else.

Is this the kind of animal I am,
always in the same trap?

His name lights
my phone, that bright artery.

In the backroom of my mind
a little movie I dim but can't shut off:

sun bouncing off creek bed, exploding
into honeysuckles on the bank.

The exclamation point
of joy at seeing

the same time I am being seen:
like a child running

full-speed downhill,
dry grass almost

cutting, sun an itch all over —
ankles and knees pumping

like drunk machinery,
light breaking

a yolk over everything
— you'll go as long as you need

to not come to the end.

PENELOPE

Each night at the loom
she picks apart the shroud grown

soft as milkweed.

All around behind shut doors
the men's faces

look like boys' catching

in the snare of sleep.
She must have imagined

each in bed, kissing

the hard vertebrae and ugly
limbs until the ugliness

was pushed under.

Finally I understand each night
as a way to be alone.

There was only one story

that did not lead directly into the heart
of a man.

She spoke it clearly

to herself, though to others
it sounded like waiting.

FOR THE WOMEN

I.

I'm curious
about your hair   where it begins —

        I'll pull it aside
clasp a necklace for you
pull a blanket to your shoulders
        move the keys
        where you won't forget.

        Hair, lashes, nipples   I
build it all. Touch
        it with my mind
        before returning the key.

Walking home with groceries,
your face steams
out of my skull.

My forward moving opens   a small wake
        of air:
        drags your name through it.

II.

Easy to see men have unstrung
themselves for you, breaths close
as an itch.

Your legs would have wrapped
around him here
where I'm sleeping.

Maybe you haven't felt a woman
vine in through your skull
shrug her negligee

to the ground
smokes on the ground
                              feet on the table.
                              Clean soft feet.

You're too polite and floss
too regularly to consider
how badly things can go.

I know how it is to be the stuttering foot
of a sewing machine.

I know how it is to finish
a man and lie

            still waiting

III.

For a time I could only iterate myself as shadow,
                              result   of another body

Light pointed at me   and I was cored

What I
            wanted required me   to stay
            very still for many years

                  How can something   like that

                  learn its own name?

IV.

The mothers wanted to be left alone.
We lay around the unheated living room, by the old piano,
by the TV console made of particleboard, too far inland
even for birds. Overhead the broad quiet
of adults not paying attention.

We bobbed in and out of each other, our lazy antennae
just checking for a pulse, days a long holler
pitched over the yellowing lawn, a page flipped
without reading. We twitched:
pill bugs shining beneath the porch's latticework.

V.

I review the details that keep the days
sliding like a greased pill.

I have been small, you understand
I have care for small things.

I dreamed a blade lisped
over my neck year after year.

Fear blared out like an intercom
speaking to no one at night.

How unanswered
I was. How shoelace tip —

how bitten tongue.

SELF-PORTRAIT AS GORDIAN KNOT

I've buried cartons of cigarettes in my chest.

And waited, minnow-dumb, for the phone to ring.

Pruning feeling like a bonsai tree, I've behaved

recursively and acted surprised every time.

My claim to fame is that I've tied the knot.

I mean: I've been the knot tied.

Another's fame is that they undid me.

SELECTION FROM THE CATALOGUE OF GAZES

I was looked at on the island of yachts and purebred dogs;
I was looked at in the sticky shadow
      of pines, surrounded
      by lines of ants that bit me;
under the hairdresser's gown, dentist's sheet,
      my hands floating above the X-ray machine like sickly wheat;
looked at in a black square of tape at the airport,
      each glance striking like hot spit on asphalt;
in the bar, I was looked at silently between the taps,
      and in the sharp stubble
      of November corn fields, in the booths
      of diners laminated with grease;
I was looked at in the mornings, slow as a bug
      while four-wheelers scalded the air;
during the friend's wedding, the friend's birthday,
      the friend's friend bumping into me in the kitchen,
      just thought they'd say hello;
and in convenience stores, by the dog food,
      by the six packs of mix-and-match beer;
looked at on the platform, having taken the night train
      in the wrong direction;
I was looked at in bed by visitors
      who sucked splinters from my palm,
      who sang to me,
      who showed me videos of them doing to others
      what they wished to do to me;
I was looked at in stirrups, sliding down to the edge of the table;
      in the tight plastic tubes of the jungle gym;
while I examined the rings of my coffee cup,
      as I thought *geological*;
looked at in a humid album laid across someone's knees;
      as the train bucked over each railroad tie
      and under a thick coat my body, and inside my body I slept;
I was looked at and told I wasn't looked at,
      as gazes followed me like a strand of unbroken syrup;

looked at and did not know it at all, as when I sliced
my finger so deeply the cells of my hand crouched
and looked at the severed cells of my finger as a sudden
stranger with another scent —

REALITIES AND CREATORS

I re-discover myself like a series
of bright pennants.

Behind me are the days without proportion:
they slam into each other, numerous

densities. When I was at the total bottom
of the cinched gunny sack

one eye stayed open, red
and kicking. Then he

came home with my specific name
nested in his tongue.

I tucked runaway
hairs behind my ear.

He fell into bed like water
breaking against a wall.

Come here, he said, with his arm
thrown out. And I did.

I ARRIVE

Faceless
as blown dandelions, solid
as a series of breaths.

The serving
bowl still wet in my hands:
I see the field–

dressed rabbit aglow
in dark grass, bound
for me, my table.

Identity a subtle knife paring
bodies apart.
Each day more is revealed

to be living:
the parts of the
parts of us.

Some days the dead
are only dead when memory
makes it so —

then fast as steam
they touch the mind.
Today I look in the window

where my faces are:
numerous
as a silver muscle

of fish. Present
as a sudden missing
blip on the radar screen.

GIRLHOOD

I was a fist
caught under my chin

in a round of Red Rover.
I was a small body

eventually startled
into a larger one.

I am no low tune
scratching into July air —

I am the lesser
part of my mother.

Still without a key:
when I stepped out

of bed each morning,
I belonged

to nothing around me.

THE FIRST STORY

My tongue was held
like a cut flower.
Packed down,

dense and small
as if saving myself
for later.

If I had a heart
it pulsed weak and
transparent as a cell.

I didn't realize
the kind of woman
I was willing to be

on my way
to becoming.
As a girl a specific myth

lodged in my ear and grew:
a woman finds her true self
only at the end of love.

A THEORY

When you're beautiful
they treat you like you're visible.
Their eyes are quiet as yellow
darts of dandelion in grass, a hallway
of high school lockers. Or their lips
float up, friendly and interested as if
here they feel safe. Suddenly you're inside
the homes, the dining room, being passed
a roll of bread. Suddenly they expect you
to answer in the same tongue.
You think of all the days before
when your loneliness was a stain
to be stepped over at the edge of the room,
when their long necks crisscrossed
above you like a canopy, keeping
their language from you.
I have, in the long solitude of my body,
asked for something else.
Even if I become the face on the magazine,
I can't forget: knowing holds,
a long low note in my chest.

AS IF TIME COULD BE NAILED TO A TREE LIKE A MAN OR A SIGN

Mosquito bites, everything
        primed for forgetting.

Who knows this better
        than the brain, the emperor.

In the night garden the voices
        — they're getting rained on.
        I hear it spreading like a wing.

I've learned to mourn
        is to dance in the proper way:
        so when I think *us*, I think clear first
        then outlines —

OK, you dropped the jar of salsa
        in the grocery store: you were doing the work
        of making sure.

I loved you like water
        held in my mouth —

loved you like the oyster
        slams its sticky foot onto a rock
        eventually.

I know I like to forget I lived,
        like to say I was a lost moon
        shining at well bottom.

But there: I had knees
        — and there: sometimes a cavity.

The smell of fresh-baked cookies

is undeniable
and I have been realer than that.

Strands of my hair fell
through the years
slowly as snow thinking its name.

Even after the last time I see you
the poem continues like a round.

TO THE ALTAR

As a girl my back
against the wall told me:
count the hearts of wolves.
Pick the wolf who pumps
blood fastest.
He will put your backpack
on the highest hook.
I dreamt of being thin
and boring as a Saltine
crusted with diamonds.
I dreamt of no work.
My heart without vantage,
lost in thickets of shoe stores
and reruns: I master advanced
breathing, so guilt evaporates
— leaves my soul pink
and tight as a drum.
At parties I know the lowest
common denominator
is discretion. I toast,
feminine as ripped stockings.
I keep climbing to the altar
to be what is burned, what is light.
Remade as pixels on a screen
chitter to each other and do not die.
I'd like to call my name back in
from the wilderness of 0s and 1s
but somewhere a row of data
sleeps like a loose fossil. I pray
to be finite, disappearing
energy. Though my eye
is tethered to light.

ACKNOWLEDGMENTS

Here is the very large family that raised me and this book, and to whom I owe some thanks. My gratitude is far longer than my book.

Thank you to my parents who gave me language and humor, grit and goodness. Thank you to my brother for being a confidante, and reminding me to be a better person.

Thank you to my teachers — you were kind to me, and taught me how to make knowledge known: Dana Townsend, Richard K. Weems, Cat Doty, Diana Goetsch, Lucy Lee, Jaimee Mirsky, Susan Rothbard, Susan L. Miller, Mark Doty, Sharon Olds, Gregory Orr for a day, Matthew Rohrer, Charles Simic, Brenda Shaughnessy, Craig Teicher, Sandra Lim, Bao Phi, Arthur Sze, and Gabrielle Calvocoressi.

Thank you to the Governor's School writers, who first showed me what a writing family could be: Lauren Clark, Daria Tavana, Dann Kessel, Zoe Rosenburg, Sarah Gelotte Sterbinsky, Will Thrower, Claire Bogan, Kate Burch, Emily Sung, Melissa Loewinger, and Lindsay D'Andrea.

Thank you to my graduate school cohort, but especially the following people for your emotional and poetry support: Cat Richardson, Lizzie Harris, Brian Trimboli, Jennifer Nelson, Abba Belgrave, Ben Purkert, Jen Levitt, Melissa Swantkowski, Alex Morris, Eric Weinstein, Peter Longofono, Morgan Parker, Sylvio Fraga, Maxine Patroni, Curtis Rogers, Sarah Holland–Batt, and Jerome Murphy.

Thank you to Kundiman, who returned a piece of myself I didn't know I was without: Elysha Chang, Jenny Xie, Vt Hung, Paul Tran, Cathy Linh Che, Sarah Gambito, and Joseph Legaspi.

Thank you to the excellent support network at Rutgers: Anna Maron, Leandra Cain, Rick H. Lee, Carolyn Williams, and Rhea Ramey.

Thank you to Deborah Landau, Adam Soldofsky, and Jessica Flynn, who made NYU a home.

Thank you to Joy Parisi and Lila Cecil for creating a place for writers, and to all the Paragraph writers for keeping me afloat — especially

Rebecca Louie.

Gratitude to these beloveds who have lent me form or helped me find
my own over the years: Allie Cislo, Jenn Eng, Justine Bienkowski, and
Stacey Balkun.

Thank you to the Vermont Studio Center, Martha's Vineyard Institute
of Creative Writing, and Geraldine R. Dodge Foundation's Poetry
Program, as well as the editors and curators who have believed in my
work over the years — particularly Alexander Weinstein and Ysabel Y.
Gonzalez.

Thank you to Jaswinder Bolina for selecting this manuscript, and to
Kate Nuernberger and Sarah Nguyen at Pleiades Press for giving this
book a body.

Thank you to Nick Macri for having been my companion.

Finally, thank you to Sujata Rajpurohit who always looks for me when
I start to disappear.

Poems in this volume previously appeared in:

Day One: "Selection from the Catalogue of Gazes"

Gulf Coast: "Orpheus, Asymptote" and "Motion, Moved"

Indiana Review: "Recovery"

The Journal: "To the Altar"

The Literary Review: "Song" and "Self-Portrait as Gordian Knot"

Narrative: "A Theory," "If I exist the equation gets more difficult," and "Summer I Didn't Have"

New England Review: "Routine"

North Dakota Quarterly: "After signing a lease on my new apartment" (published under the title "Leda & Other Women") and "For the Women"

Pleiades: "I Arrive" (published under the title "Late Self")

Slice Magazine: "Nearly"

Southeast Review: "He tells me: Come back when you've pried yourself open." and "As if time could be nailed to a tree like a man or a sign."

Sycamore Review: "On Distance"

The Offing: "Permission," "After Maine," and "Good is what you become when you think someone is looking."

Wreck Park: "Inside-Out Joke"

ABOUT THE AUTHOR

Amy Meng is a Kundiman Fellow and poetry editor at *Bodega Magazine*, as well as a 2016 Amy Award winner. Her poetry has appeared in *Day One*, *Gulf Coast*, *Indiana Review*, *Narrative Magazine*, and the *New England Review*, among others. She currently lives in Brooklyn.

THE LENA-MILES WEVER TODD PRIZE

The editors at Pleiades Press select 10–15 finalists from among those manuscripts submitted each year. An external judge selects one winner for publication. All selections are made blind to authorship in in an open competition for which any poet writing in English is eligible. Lena-Miles Wever Todd Prize for Poetry books are distributed by Louisiana State University Press.

ALSO AVAILABLE FROM PLEIADES PRESS

A Lesser Love by E. J. Koh

In Between: Poetry Comics by Mita Mahato

Novena by Jacques J. Rancourt

Book of No Ledge: Visual Poems by Nance Van Winckel

Landscape with Headless Mama by Jennifer Givhan

Random Exorcisms by Adrian C. Louis

Poetry Comics from the Book of Hours by Bianca Stone

The Belle Mar by Katie Bickham

Sylph by Abigail Cloud

The Glacier's Wake by Katy Didden

Paradise, Indiana by Bruce Snider

What's this, Bombardier? by Ryan Flaherty

Self-Portrait with Expletives by Kevin Clark

Pacific Shooter by Susan Parr

It was a terrible cloud at twilight by Alessandra Lynch

Compulsions of Silkworms & Bees by Julianna Baggott

Snow House by Brian Swann

Motherhouse by Kathleen Jesme

Lure by Nils Michals

PLEIADES
P R E S S